Echoes Of A Dying Society's Heartbeat

A collection of poems

by Kaleef Lloyd

Echoes Of A Dying Society's Heartbeat

Copyright © 2022 by Kaleef Lloyd

ISBN: 9798843208394

For information contact:
Kaleef Lloyd,
www.beanththeleef.com

Book and Cover design by

Kaleef Lloyd & Nayani Mora-Lloyd

Editor: Kariana Mora-Lloyd

This book would not have been possible without my high school teacher Mr. Murphy who turned my hatred of poetry into a passion. Thank you to my family and friends who took the time read my work.

"Our differences don't keep us apart
It's believing our differences keep us apart does." -
KML

Table Of Contents

We Say Thoughts & Prayers

We all watched in horror
as leaves and branches
turned into piles
of smoldering ash

Tiny white particles
flooded the space
and showered them
With soot, then
Heart breaking cries
For help flooded the airwaves

Not one single person
budged from their chair
Stricken with fear
and self-preservation
Everyone looked down
Said thoughts and prayers
Then turned the channel

Empath's Remorse

The scars left from
Everyone's words
Formed like little
bite marks on her head

She unwillingly
carried their disappointment,
Hatred and bitterness

At the same time
She couldn't help
To absorb their fear
Their sadness

The scars would be
a reminder of
her naivety

But she still
Desired to heal them
So, their suffering
Would end together

Fake Love

The love you gave everyone was counterfeit.
Now they have to pay the bill
For your fakeness
With left over change from your trust issues

Greedy Optimists

I found it clinging
To us for dear life
It was our hope
Dreams, the future,
But our selfish needs
Caused it to slip away

The Forgotten Human Being

I wrapped myself
in a blanket of yesterday's regrets

Tomorrow's excuses
and today's bad decisions
then someone called me

The constant ringing annoyed me
but reminded me that I am loved

Corrupt Philosophers

They spun your truth
To fit their lies
To justify their swelling bank accounts
Unknowingly, their lies would doom us all.

Unacceptable Truths

We were both driven

By the illusions of peace

The truth hit our souls like missiles

And nearly sank our beliefs

For a better tomorrow but hope still

Lingered in our aching heart

For the next generation

To end the war on ourselves.

Life Savior

I reached out

To touch the surface

Of your heart

But ended up

Almost drowning

In your sorrow

Before finding

My way back

To the shore

Colonizers

It started with trimming
Her branches

Carefully snipping away
the twigs and fruits
she bore for us

She seemed happy to give
The more she gave,
The more we would take
Until nothing else was left
.
So, we cut and stripped away
Her memories and dignity

We tore up her roots
Replotted the land
For her rebirth
To fit what we wanted.

With high hopes we replanted her
But the new version of her
Grew back hallow of love
And compassion
Just like us

Grateful

We both fell

Victim to the charm

Of tomorrow

Without taking in consideration

Of The gifts presented

To us today.

Broken Boundary

We drilled holes that

Run deep towards your core

Until we hit graves

Filled with failed

Dreams of others

Even though you fought back

We found more ways to destroy you

A handful of us look towards the stars

Others just want to heal you

Unfortunately, we are the source of your pain

Reverse High Maintenance

You shrunk
Your standards
And ended up
Paying for the
Shortcomings
With your dignity

Birthday Party

The 40th cycle was the hardest
Every day, I found pieces
Of the old you
In the books.
Always wondering
If I could go back in tine
To get back
Your natural beauty.
How could I be sympathetic to you
When I spent 30 years being
The root of your pain

Game Masters

18

We thought you
Would last forever
Silly us
You just played
The game longer

Ripple Effects

Our wandering minds
Meet in the sea
The noise of crashing waves
Draw me to you
It felt like fate
My destiny
Would be tied
To your wellness
My wellness would
Be tied to you
Let us both be comforted
By the moment
By each other's presence
As we wander the beach together

Character Assassins

They came armed with words
Of soul crushing destruction.

The character assassin didn't desire peace
They only sought the satisfaction
Of damaging someone's spirit

Our only shield against such deliberate unprovoked hate
Was to kill them with kindness.

Earthbound Love

It was easy for you
To bend me
To your will

Everything about you
Captivated me

Just the thought of you
Provided me with comfort

You unintentionally groomed me
Like many of your other lovers
Who became fascinated
With you being you

When I needed more
Your silence
Provided me
With an unexplained
Sense of gratification

It was how our relationship worked
You were always there with me
For better or worse
Even when I couldn't be there
For you

As they buried my body
I felt at peace
Knowing I would be
Part of you forever.

Offspring

I flung myself
Out of the door
Unclog my mind
From reality and thoughts
I just wanted to enjoy the fall
From grace like you did.

Cultural Inheritance

The disbelief on our faces was evident.
Our actions destroyed the only one who cared
About all of us.

With heavy hearts we buried
Our last connection to the past, future, and soul.

Kindness Spreader

The lies I told myself
Betrayed my spirit
I feed my selfish desires
Which cause my soul
To spoil faster than milk
And heart to rot
But you healed me
With your undying love
You had nothing to gain
But everything to lose
You left without asking for
Thank you
Just a note telling me
To pay the kindness
Forward.

Global Warming

We recognize
Your suffering
Our failure to listen
Is leading to your demise
Now is the time
We will work together
The problem is we're already too late

Human Nature

Within a blink
Of an eye
Our entire view
Of the world changed

All you wanted
Was to provide
A safe place
For us

But we couldn't
Fight our nature
For destruction

Our desire
To out do
Each other.

You pay the price
For checks
You didn't want cashed

King's Remedy

He built the foundation
Of his kingdom
On everyone's hatred

Community's Child

We caused her
To erupt with
Unscripted joy
Just saying
The words
You matter
Broke past her
Mental Block
Her Depression
To fill the
Forgotten Space
In her heart
That was once
Home to love
Now she will
Reap the benefits
Of feeling loved again

Heart Controller

My eyes were griped by your beauty

It made me question my place in the universe

There was nothing quite like you

You wore your emotions on your sleeve

And I was your yo-yo.

Celebrity Status

I rediscovered
My imagination
And got rekindled
With my dreams
Of making everything
Around me better

In this world
Everything loved
Me for being me

But even here
I can't protect myself
From the disappointment
And grief of failing
To protect you

While others destroyed
Your character
For I knew the real you
They only know the person
Behind the social handle

Tales of the self-absorbed

We suffer from the loss of your trust

Each day we feel the pain of our actions

We broke your heart and left you

To feel the weight of our regret

Abusers

She had a way
Of challenging us
That made us fight
For her very being
Everyone wanted her
It didn't matter
How we got her
We killed
We lie
We cheat
We did whatever
It took
Then we got her
But, found out
She was really never ours

Narcissistic Regret

We took everything
From each other
Battled for the scraps
It was always life or death

Either I get you
Or you get me

The mentality was ingrained
In us from the very beginning

When we finally depart the earth
And look back on it all

We have to ask
Was it worth it?

No One Wins

The sweet pulsating sounds
Of your hands clapping
Made me smile

It was a sign
That you were happy
Then you started
Moving towards
His direction

I felt jealousy rise
Further and further
Past my heart
Until it reached my brain

Rage slowly built inside me
It felt like a volcano erupted
When I shot him my most evil look

But both failed to see it
So, I started planning ways
To take them down.

Happiness Unlocked

The strong but satisfying death

Of her emotions created a stoic

Unmoving, unnerving

She sought the small joys

Of Memes to help her crack a smile

Caste Climber

Every mountain he climbed changed him

Each obstacle he overcame

Lead to an uncharted territory within himself

Undiscovered emotions and mementos from the past

Made him realize how much he changed

From a young man who lived in a subway station

To looking down on people as he topped his version

Of the world where everyone lay beneath him.

True Selves

The danger of losing

Everything that made us, us

Made us stand still

As a mirror was help up

To show us who really are as society.

World Changer

They broke him into pieces

Without a care In the world

Each layer of protection was destroyed

Along with his desire to love.

But he couldn't give up on them

So, he snatched up

The shattered pieces of his soul

To put himself back together again

Deep Self

You play victim for rewards

You never understood who you

Hurt in the process

But the bags you carry full of expensive shoes

Are getting heaver with future regret,

Generation Unforeseen

The promises we made to you
Sparked a revolution
No one quite expected
For you, it was long overdue
For us, it was acceptance.

Equality was an illusion
And they played the role of magician well

The greedy gatekeepers
Blocked access to our birthright
And made it invite only

Our actions were deemed
Unholy by people who never met us
We were an abomination
Our right to choose
Our right for freedom meant nothing

Meanwhile, their exclusive private party
Was in for a rude awakening.

We released ourselves
From the mental bondages
Built to keep us in check
With our minds focused on building
A bridge of togetherness amongst
Broken communities everywhere
Driven by one goal,
To create better world for you

It's A Woman's World

They tried to fix her
But brought the wrong tools
For the job
She in turned rebuilt their point of view

Shadow Love

He follows me wherever I go
Always chasing my movements
And mimicking everything I did
He idolized me

But I wasn't supposed be his savior
I was a ghost of my former self
It didn't stop him for worshipping me

The only time he left me alone was at night
When I wanted his attention the most

City Life

The lights blinded us
Turned us into Consumer Zombies

Without a care in the world
We devoured each other's humanity

To claim a piece of land
That was never ours to begin with

Social Dissonance

It exposed the passion
We have for ourselves

Tik tock, tik, tock
The constant ticking
Invaded and expanded
Our minds at the same time

The hunger for more of it
Made us ignore our real problems
As the world crumbled all around us

Peace Brokers

When we met at the end
Of the table

The stakes were never higher
Feuds must be settled

Healing must be the goal
For us to enjoy a future of unity

No Light Is Complete Without Darkness

Time matters above all
We can't experience joy
Without the presence of pain
Negative and positive experiences
Must operate on the same plane
It's your choice to funnel your energy
Into one or the other and not dwell
On the imbalance caused by universe

Loss Faith

Nothing hits harder
Then the piercing bite
Of disappointment
Knowing we failed
Each other.

The Healing Process

Jealously wreaked havoc
On her mind, until regret
Filled the space and her
Hate faded into sadness

Divine Intervention

Instant sadness came over me
As I watched the little boy cry
And chase after his red balloon

Each time he jumped
It slipped out his of reach

The higher it traveled
He became more determined
To get what was rightfully his back
Even as tears streamed across his face

Just as he started running out of breath
A stranger grabbed the balloon from the sky
Give it to the boy, then left

My only thought as I carried
An eagerness to jump over the bridge
Was to not give up as I looked down
At the suicide help number, before making a call

One World Named Pangea

Our worlds are split into many halves
The further away our halves drift apart
It stops us from seeing how whole
We once were many moons ago.